Improve y
sight-reading!

Paul Harris

FABER *ff* MUSIC

Introduction

Being a good sight-reader is so important and it's not difficult at all! If you work through this book carefully – always making sure that you really understand each exercise before you play it – you'll never have problems learning new pieces or doing well at sight-reading in exams!

Using the workbook

1 Rhythmic exercises

Make sure you have grasped these fully before you go on to the melodic exercises: it is vital that you really know how the rhythms work. There are a number of ways to do the exercises, several of which are outlined in Stage 1. Try them all out. Can you think of more ways to do them?

2 Melodic exercises

These exercises use just the notes (and rhythms) for the Stage, and progress gradually. If you want to sight-read fluently and accurately, get into the simple habit of working through each exercise in the following ways before you begin to play it:

- Make sure you understand the rhythm and counting. Clap the exercise through.
- Know what notes you are going to play and the fingering you are going to use.
- Try to hear the piece through in your head. Always play the first note to help.

3 Prepared pieces

Work your way through the questions first, as these will help you to think about, or 'prepare' the piece. Don't begin playing until you are pretty sure you know exactly how the piece goes.

4 Going solo!

It is now up to you to discover the clues in this series of practice pieces. Give yourself about a minute and do your best to understand the piece before you play. Check the rhythms and fingering, and try to hear the piece in your head.

Always remember to feel the pulse and to keep going steadily once you've begun.

Good luck and happy sight-reading!

Terminology:
Bar = measure

Grade 1   Stage 1

C major

Rhythmic exercises

Always practise the rhythmic exercises carefully first. There are different ways
of doing these exercises:

• Your teacher (or a metronome) taps the lower line while you clap or tap
  the upper line.
• You tap the lower line with your foot and clap or tap the upper line.
• You tap one line with one hand and the other line with the other hand on
  a table top or any flat surface.
• You tap the lower line and sing the upper line.

Before you begin each exercise count two bars in – one out loud and one silently.

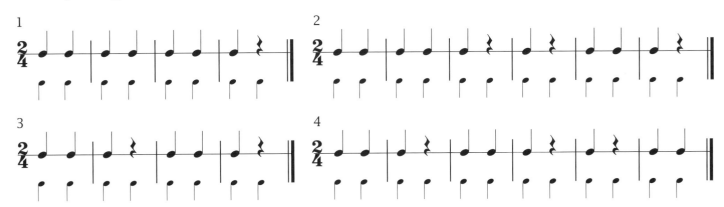

Melodic exercises

Hear each exercise in your head before you play it.

Prepared pieces

1 How many beats are there in each bar? Count six bars aloud, clapping the pulse at the same time.

2 What is the key? Play the first five notes of the scale, ascending and descending.

3 What do bars 2 and 3 have in common?

4 Play a C (the first note), then hear the piece in your head.

5 How will you put some character into your performance?

Heavily

1 What does $\frac{2}{4}$ mean? What is the $\frac{2}{4}$ marking called?

2 On a flat surface, tap the pulse with one hand and the rhythm with the other.

3 Are there any repeated patterns?

4 Compare the note in bar 3 with the first note in bar 4.

5 How will you put some character into your performance?

Lightly

Improvise!

Improvise a 4-bar tune, then a 6-bar tune beginning with these two bars.

Compose!

Compose your own 4-bar tune beginning with these two bars – make the final note a C. Then play your tune.

Going solo!

Talk about each piece before you play it. Mention note names, scale
and rhythmic patterns, and the character. After you've played it,
consider how well the music matched your description.

Grade 1   Stage 2

Rhythmic exercises

Always remember to count two bars in.

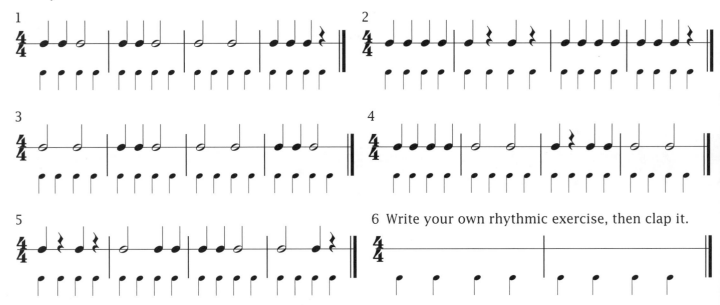

6 Write your own rhythmic exercise, then clap it.

Melodic exercises

Set 1: Not including B♭

Set 2: Including B♭

Prepared pieces

1 How many beats are there in each bar? Count six bars aloud, clapping the pulse at the same time.

2 What is the key? Can you find any scale patterns?

3 Play the highest and lowest notes. What are their names?

4 Play an F (the first note), then hear the piece in your head. Try singing the first two bars.

5 How will you play this piece 'expressively'?

1 What does ⁴⁄₄ mean? Hear a ⁴⁄₄ pulse in your head.

2 Tapping the pulse, hear the rhythm silently in your head. Then, clap the rhythm and tap the pulse with a foot at the same time.

3 Are there any repeated rhythmic patterns?

4 In which key is this piece? Find the note affected by the key signature.

5 How will you make the piece sound like a march?

Improvise!

Improvise a 4-bar tune, then a 6-bar tune beginning with these two bars:

Compose!

Compose your own 4-bar tune beginning with these two bars. Use some patterns or ideas from the opening bars and make the final note F. Then play your tune.

Going solo!

Read through each piece carefully before you play it, hearing it in
your head as best you can. Then, count in two bars and think about
how you continue to feel the pulse once you've begun.

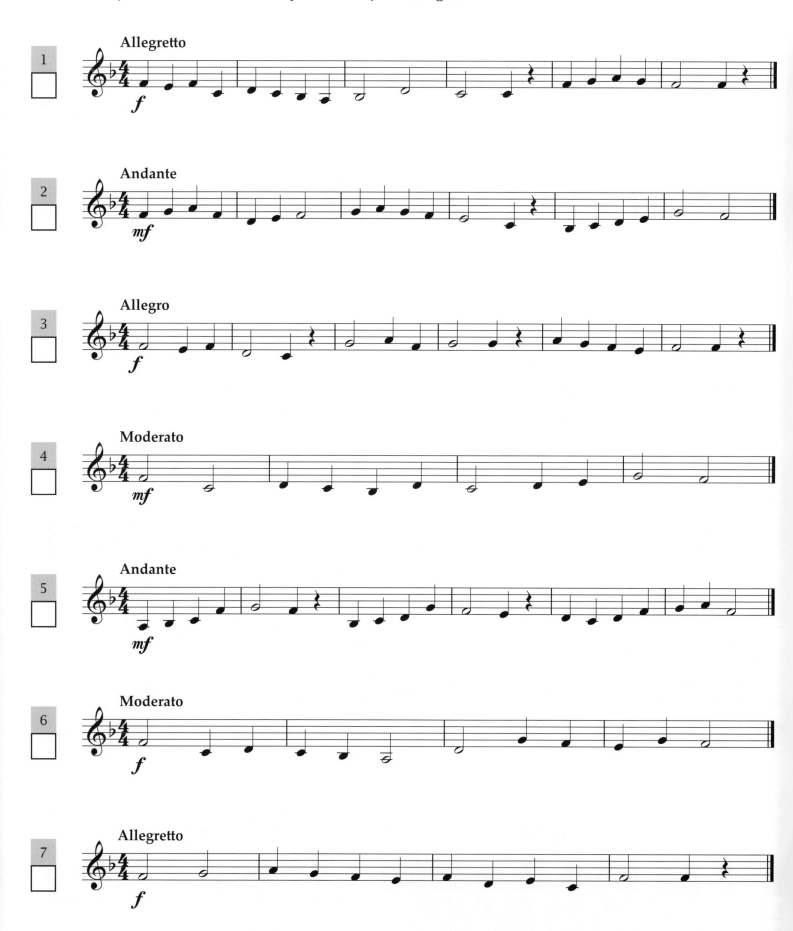

Grade 1   Stage 3

Rhythmic exercises

Always remember to count two bars in.

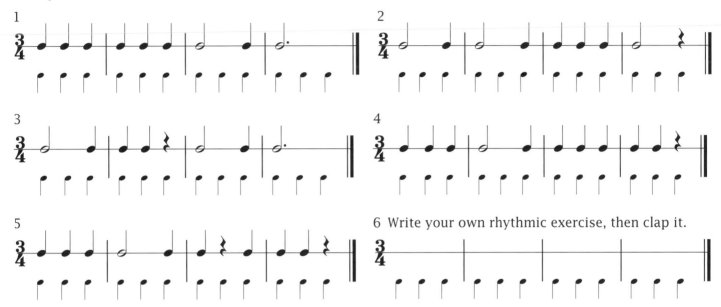

6 Write your own rhythmic exercise, then clap it.

Melodic exercises

Set 1: Not including F♯

Set 2: Including F♯

Prepared pieces

1 What does the time signature tell you? Count six bars aloud, clapping the pulse at the same time.

2 What is the key? Play the scale, thinking the note names as you play them.

3 Play the highest and lowest notes. What are their names?

4 Play a G (the first note), then hear the piece in your head. Now try singing the first four bars.

5 How will you play this piece gently?

1 What dance is in ¾ time? Count six bars of ¾, clapping on the 1st and 3rd beat of each bar.

2 Tapping the pulse, hear the rhythm silently in your head. Then, clap the rhythm and tap the pulse with a foot at the same time.

3 Can you find an almost-complete scale pattern?

4 Why does G major have an F♯?

5 How will you make this piece sound happy?

Improvise!

Improvise a 4-bar tune, then a 6-bar tune beginning with these two bars.

Compose!

Compose your own 4-bar tune beginning with these two bars. Use some patterns or ideas from the opening bars and make the final note G. Then play your tune.

Going solo!

Think about what 'playing with character' means. How can you play each of these pieces with character? Choose two bars from each piece and use them to begin an improvisation – play it with character.

Grade 1   Stage 4

Rhythmic exercises

6 Write your own rhythmic exercise, then clap it.

Melodic exercises

Prepared pieces

1 What are quavers? Explain how you will count them. Counting the pulse
   aloud, tap the rhythm.

2 What is the key? Play the scale, thinking of the note names as you play them.

3 Find all the notes affected by the key signature and think of them in a
   different colour.

4 Play a G (the first note), then hear the piece in your head. Now try singing the
   first two bars.

5 What does *Andante* mean? Which words best describe the character: angry,
   flowing, thoughtful, ghostly?

1

1 Can you find two bars with the same rhythm?

2 Count four bars of $\frac{3}{4}$ aloud, then continue counting silently and tap the
   rhythm of the piece.

3 Play the arpeggio of the key. Can you find an arpeggio pattern in this piece?

4 Are any notes affected by the key signature?

5 How will you make the piece sound grand?

2

Improvise!

Improvise a 4-bar tune, then a 6-bar tune,
beginning with these two bars.

Compose!

Compose your own 4-bar tune beginning with these two bars. Use some patterns or ideas from
the opening bars and make the final note F. Add dynamic marks, a tempo word and slurs.

Going solo!

Choose a bar from your chosen piece. Study it for about half a minute,
then play it from memory. When you are confident, repeat this activity,
trying to memorise two bars.

Grade 2 Stage 1

Ties

Rhythmic exercises

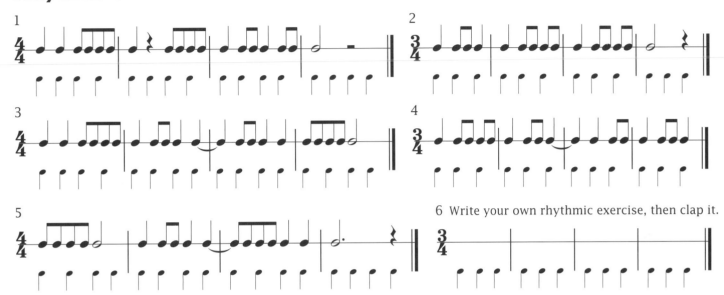

6 Write your own rhythmic exercise, then clap it.

Melodic exercises

Set 1:

Set 2: Simple ties

Prepared pieces

> **1** What is a tied note? Find the tied notes in this piece, then tap or clap bars 5–8.
>
> **2** What is the key? Play the scale, thinking of the note names as you play them.
>
> **3** Can you find any repeated rhythm patterns? Tapping the pulse with a foot, clap the rhythm of the whole piece.
>
> **4** Play a C (the first note), then hear the piece in your head as best you can.
>
> **5** What does 'Minuet' mean? How will you give the piece a 'Minuet' character?

> **1** What is the character of this piece? What are the clues?
>
> **2** Find the two sets of ties then tap bars 5–8.
>
> **3** Count two bars of 4/4 aloud, then continue counting silently and clap or tap the rhythm.
>
> **4** In which key is this piece? Make up a little tune in the key.
>
> **5** Play a C (the first note), then hear the piece in your head as best you can, with character.

Improvise!

Improvise a 4-bar tune, then a 6-bar tune, beginning with these two bars.

Compose!

Compose your own 4-bar tune beginning with these two bars. Use some patterns or ideas from the opening bars and make the final note a C. Add dynamic marks, a tempo word and slurs.

Going solo!

Before playing the piece describe, with as much detail as possible, what you see.
Mention key, melodic shapes and patterns, rhythm (particularly quaver patterns and
tied notes), repeated rhythmic patterns, dynamics and character.

Grade 2 Stage 2

A minor

Rhythmic exercises

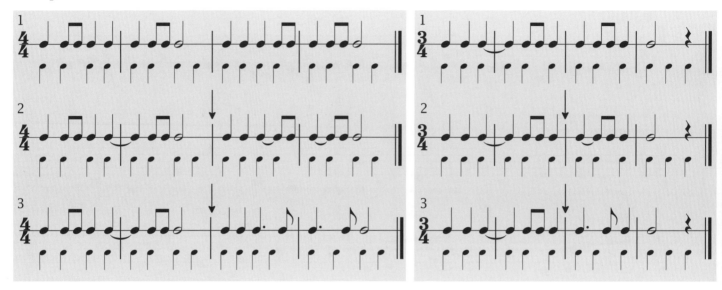

Melodic exercises

Set 1: A minor   What do A minor and C major have in common?

Set 2:

Feel the 4th beat strongly in this tune.

Feel the 2nd beat strongly in this one.

Prepared pieces

1 In which key is this piece? What is the relative major?

2 Describe the ♩. ♪ pattern. How will you count it?

3 Can you find any repeated rhythm patterns?

4 Tapping the pulse with a foot, clap the rhythm of the whole piece. In bars that contain dotted rhythms, which beat is it important to feel strongly?

5 What does '*Cantabile*' mean? How will you give the piece character?

1 What is the character of the piece? Why is it important to follow the dynamic markings?

2 How many times does the rhythm in bar 2 repeat? Tap a pulse with a foot and clap this bar.

3 Count two bars in ¾ aloud, then continue counting silently and clap or tap the rhythm of the whole piece.

4 In which key is this piece? Play a two-octave scale in the key, then make up a little tune in the key.

5 Play the key note, then hear the piece in your head as best you can, with all the dynamic markings.

Improvise and compose!

Make up your own piece beginning with this bar and write it down on manuscript paper. Decide on a mood or character before you begin.

Going solo!

Study the piece for about half a minute, then, with the music out of sight,
make up a piece with broadly similar rhythmic and melodic shapes.

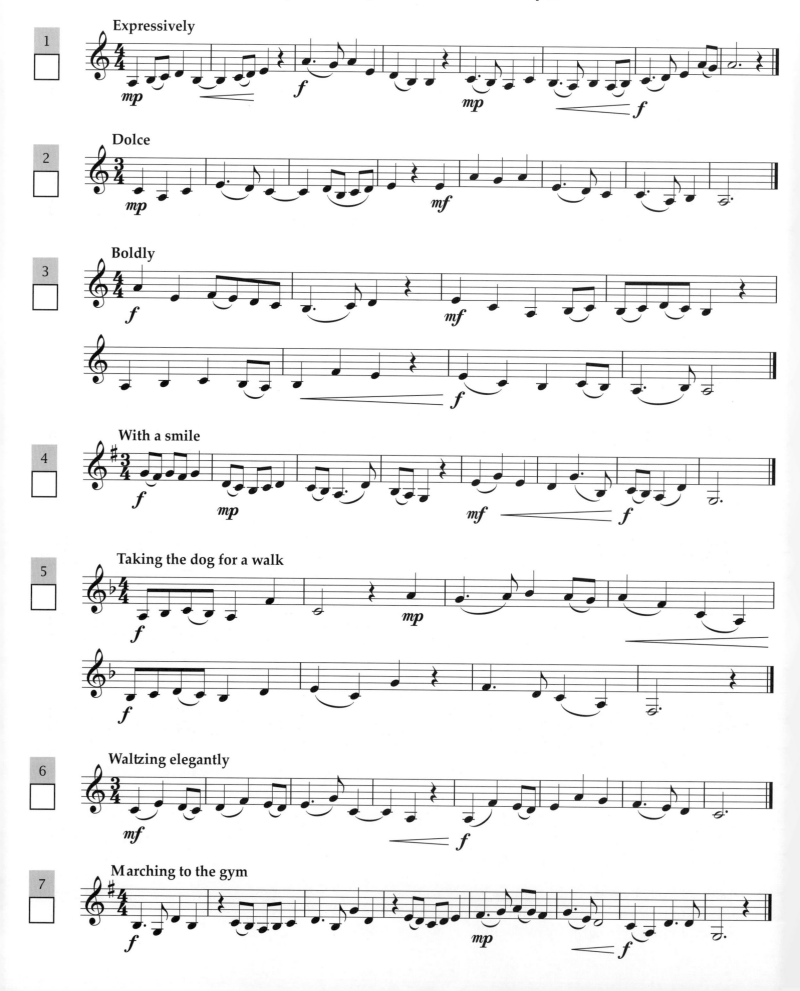

Grade 2 Stage 3

Rhythmic exercises

Melodic exercises

Prepared pieces

> **1** In which key is this piece? Play the scale and arpeggio, then look for any
>   bars based on those patterns.
>
> **2** What is *staccato*? How will you play notes marked *staccato*?
>
> **3** Can you find any repeated rhythm patterns?
>
> **4** Tapping the pulse with a foot, clap the rhythm of the whole piece.
>
> **5** How will you give the piece character? Play the first note, then hear the
>   piece in your head – hear the character too.

> **1** What is the character of this piece? What are the clues?
>
> **2** In which key is the piece? Play a one-octave scale in this key.
>
> **3** Count two bars of $\frac{4}{4}$ aloud, then continue counting silently and clap or
>   tap the rhythm of the whole piece.
>
> **4** Give the piece a running commentary, mentioning rhythms, melodic
>   patterns and markings.
>
> **5** Play an A (the key note), then hear the piece in your head as best you
>   can, with all the dynamic markings.

Improvise and compose!

Make up your own piece beginning with this bar
and write it down on manuscript paper. Decide on
a mood or character before you begin.

Going solo!

Are there any bars where you couldn't clap the rhythm instantly? If there are,
think about them, work them out and then clap these rhythms before you play.

Grade 2   Stage 4

Rhythmic exercises

Make up your own 4-bar rhythms that include these patterns,
then clap them. Finally, improvise a melody to fit your rhythms.

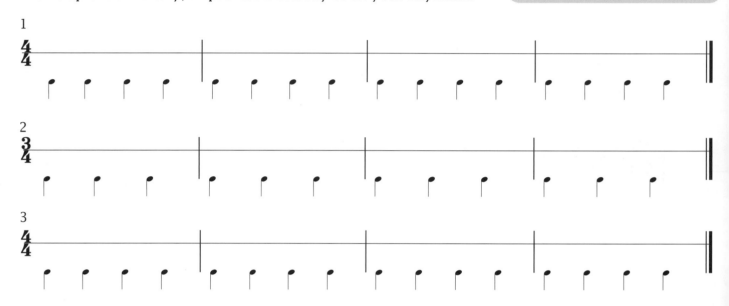

Melodic exercises

Prepared pieces

1 In which key is this piece? Play the scale and arpeggio, then look for any bars based on those patterns.

2 Do any bars have the same patterns?

3 What is a *crescendo*? Practice playing bar 2 with a very clear *crescendo*.

4 Tapping the pulse with one hand on a flat surface, clap the rhythm of the whole piece with the other hand.

5 How will you give the piece character? Play the first note, then hear the piece in your head – hear the character too.

1 What is the character of this piece? What are the clues?

2 What will you do to be sure the dotted rhythms are accurate?

3 Count two bars of $\frac{3}{4}$ aloud, then continue counting silently and clap or tap the rhythm of the whole piece.

4 Give the piece a running commentary, mentioning rhythms, melodic patterns, and markings.

5 Play a B♭ (the first note), then hear the piece in your head as best you can, with all the dynamic markings.

Improvise and compose!

Make up your own piece beginning with this bar and write in down on manuscript paper. Decide on a mood or character before you begin.

Going solo!

Think about what 'playing with character' means. How can you bring a sense of character to each piece you play? What ingredients are you going to make use of?

Grade 3   Stage 1

4-note slurs

Rhythmic exercises

Melodic exercises

Prepared pieces

> **1** Look through this piece, do you feel you really understand it?
>
> **2** Are you certain of all the rhythms?
>
> **3** Play the appropriate scale first at *p*, then at *f*. Then, play with a *crescendo* on the way up and a *diminuendo* on the way down.
>
> **4** Play the first note, then hear the piece in your head as best you can, with all the musical expression.
>
> **5** How will you give the piece character?

1

Gracefully

> **1** What is the character of this piece? What are the clues?
>
> **2** Set a pulse in your mind, then sub-divide the pulse into 2 and 4. How does this relate to the first bar?
>
> **3** Count two bars of ¾ aloud, then continue counting silently and clap or tap the rhythm of the whole piece.
>
> **4** Give the piece a running commentary, mentioning rhythms, melodic patterns, and markings.
>
> **5** Play a C, then study bars 5 and 6 for a few moments. Hear them in your head, then try to play them from memory.

2

Playfully

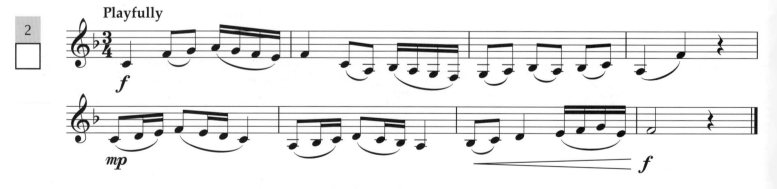

Improvise and compose!

Make up your own piece beginning with this bar and write it down on manuscript paper. Decide on a mood or character before you begin.

Going solo!

In each piece think about the first dynamic marking and how it relates to those
that follow. Make sure that the different markings are *really* contrasted.

Grade 3   Stage 2

D minor

Rhythmic exercises

Melodic exercises

Which tune is in F major? How are D minor and F major related?

Prepared pieces

1 Look through this piece. Do you feel you really understand it?

2 Each phrase is two bars long, how will you make this clear in your performance?

3 Play the appropriate scale first at *mf*, then at *f*.

4 Play the first note, then hear the piece in your head, with all the musical expression.

5 How will you give the piece character?

1 How much of this piece is based on scale patterns?

2 Set a pulse in your mind, then sub-divide the pulse into 2 and 4. How does this relate to the first bar?

3 Count two bars of $\frac{3}{4}$ aloud, then continue counting silently and tap the rhythm of the whole piece.

4 Give the piece a running commentary, mentioning rhythms, melodic patterns, and markings.

5 Play a D, then study bars 1 and 2 for a few moments. Hear them in your head, then try to play them from memory.

Improvise and compose!

Make up your own piece beginning with this phrase and write it down on manuscript paper.

Now compose a piece in D minor, including the ♪. ♪ pattern. Remember to write it down.

Going solo!

Before you play each piece, choose a single bar, study it for a few seconds,
then play it from memory.

Grade 3   Stage 3

Rhythmic exercises

Melodic exercises

Prepared pieces

1 What does $\frac{3}{8}$ mean? How do you count in $\frac{3}{8}$?

2 In which key is this piece? Can you spot any scale and arpeggio patterns?

3 Play the scale at all three dynamic markings in the piece.

4 Play the first note, then hear the piece in your head, with all the musical expression.

5 How will you give the piece character?

1

1 In which key is this piece? Why is there a C♯ in bar 3?

2 How will you make sure that bar 6 is accurate?

3 Count two bars of $\frac{3}{8}$ aloud, then continue counting silently and tap the rhythm of the whole piece.

4 Which note is affected by the key signature?

5 Play a D (the key note), then study the first two bars for a few moments. Hear them in your head, then try to play them from memory.

2

Improvise and compose!

Make up your own piece (it can be as long or short as you like), beginning with this phrase and write it down on manuscript paper.

1

2 Now compose another piece, including as many $\frac{3}{8}$ patterns as you can. Remember to write it down.

Going solo!

Think about counting in quavers. Clap the rhythm of each piece before you play it.

Grade 3   Stage 4

Rhythmic exercises

Melodic exercises

Prepared pieces

1 How will you ensure the semiquavers in bar 5 are in time?

2 In which key is this piece? Find the notes affected by the key signature.

3 Set a crotchet pulse and play the scale first in quavers and then in semiquavers.

4 Play the first note, then hear the piece in your head, with all the musical expression.

5 Which word best describes the piece: dance, dirge, dolce, or driven?

1 In which key is this piece? Why are there G♯s in bar 3 and 7?

2 What do you call the pattern that makes up the first three notes?

3 Count two bars of $\frac{3}{8}$ aloud, then continue counting silently and tap the rhythm of the whole piece.

4 What do the *staccato* notes add to the piece?

5 Hear the piece as best you can in your head. Then play it with absolute confidence.

Improvise and compose!

Make up your own piece (it can be as long or short as you like), beginning with this phrase and write it down on manuscript paper.

Now compose another piece using your own idea. Remember to write it down.

Going solo!

After you've played each piece evaluate your performance in a very objective
manner. Avoid comments like: 'That wasn't very good, I played it badly.' If there
were any slips, think about how you will put them right, and play it again.

The golden rules

A sight-reading checklist

1 Look at the time signature and decide how you will count the piece.

2 Look at the key signature and think about how to finger the notes.

3 Notice patterns – especially those based on scales and arpeggios.

4 Notice any markings that will help you convey the character.

5 Count at least one bar in.

When performing a sight-reading piece

1 Keep feeling the pulse.

2 Keep going at a steady tempo.

3 Remember *to think in key*.

4 Ignore slips.

5 Look ahead – at least to the next note.

6 Play musically, always trying to convey the character of the music.

Look at each piece for about half a minute and try to feel that you *understand* what you see (just like reading these words). Don't begin until you think you are going to play the piece accurately.

I would like to express many thanks to Tom Dent, Jean Cockburn and Jonathan Howse

© 2017 by Faber Music Ltd
Bloomsbury House, 74–77 Great Russell Street, London WC1B 3DA
Music setting by Donald Thomson
Cover and page design by Susan Clarke
Printed in England by Caligraving Ltd
All rights reserved

ISBN10: 0-571-53987-4
EAN13: 978-0-571-53987-1

To buy Faber Music publications or to find out about the full range of titles available
please contact your local music retailer or Faber Music sales enquiries:
Faber Music Ltd, Burnt Mill, Elizabeth Way, Harlow CM20 2HX
Tel: +44 (0) 1279 82 89 82   Fax: 44 (0) 1279 82 89 83
sales@fabermusic.com   fabermusicstore.com